Drive To Success: Mastering The Art of Auto Sales and Vehicle Exchange.

Jinetta Brown

Dedication

To my loving family, whose unwavering support has been the backbone of my journey—this book is for you. To my husband, whose love and patience have illuminated every chapter, guiding me through the writing process.

I also dedicate this work to all those who dare to dream, believe, and persevere. May this book inspire you and elevate your career to new heights.

A special mention to Cedric, a true intercessor in my life. His dream about me encouraged me to embark on this writing journey, reminding me that the call to create is often a divine whisper.

Acknowledgment

I would like to acknowledge the silent stars—those who never had a voice in the room but had so much to say. This book is also dedicated to those who were overlooked for promotions they truly deserved. And to my haters, thank you for being my motivators.

A heartfelt thank you to my sister, who's been my Irish twin since day one. Your love and support mean the world to me. My mother, who is the reason behind my existence, always believed in me. You are my support; I love you.

I extend my deepest gratitude to everyone who contributed to the creation of this book. A special thanks goes to my mentor, whose invaluable guidance and feedback have been instrumental in shaping this manuscript.

I also want to acknowledge my cousins, Keith and Renee, for their support and encouragement throughout this journey. Much love always.

Finally, I want to emphasize that this is the first book written by a woman about auto sales and vehicle exchange, and I hope it paves the way for others in the industry.

About the Author

I am originally from Illinois, and throughout my life, I have always loved helping and encouraging others. But somewhere along the way, things that started good often turned bad. Well, not anymore.

I created my own lane and found my voice in the room—for those who have been counted out or overlooked. You are now in a judgment-free zone, and this is your safe platform.

It is a blessing to be a blessing. Enjoy the book and know that what you read here is the truth—it will educate and motivate you in the right way. Always remember: you control your own destiny.

Now I can train the world, sharing knowledge and insights to empower others.

It's not about how you start, but how you finish.

With love,

Jinetta Brown

(Author and Friend Forever)

Contents

Chapter 1: Introduction

"People can miss the tackle in a thousand ways, but if you show them the right way, they will never miss it again."

We often need a guide, a path revealed to us to move forward and achieve success. Although there's no shortcut to success, it is a blessing when we are guided the right way at the right time. After 20 years in the car business, I have found considerable success and made my mark in this field. As an African-American woman—a rare sight in this industry—I learned to pave my own way and have received several accolades, such as presidential awards, and have been nationally ranked as a salesperson of the month, both in the city and the district. I have been diligent in my strategies as a salesperson, earning over $3 million in the car business.

My beloved late husband, whom I lost to pancreatic cancer just before the pandemic struck, was my biggest supporter. He would call me the "princess of cars" because of how far I had come. Unfortunately, fate did not allow him to stay with me despite my countless prayers. My prayers felt unheard as he battled cancer for five years before he was gone. Losing someone so close feels like losing a part of yourself, completely altering your life.

At this point, you may wonder why I am writing this book. The idea for creating a guide to the vehicle exchange program emerged when the auctions were closed due to COVID-19. Cars became hard to find, especially through auctions during the pandemic. This situation inspired me to develop a program where used cars would be made more accessible to consumers who typically do not come from auctions. The goal was for consumers to see, touch, and feel the used cars in person while accessing the service records. This way, they could better gauge the condition of the vehicles instead of purchasing them online without the opportunity to inspect them firsthand.

Every success I have achieved has been driven by a strategic mindset akin to a formula that has consistently proven fruitful. This is why I am writing this book—as a manual for readers who want to accelerate their success in the automobile business. If you are interested in the dealership and want to add an extra hundred dollars to your monthly earnings, then you must continue reading to learn the formula for succeeding in this field.

In this part of the world, I have realized that there isn't much written about a success formula. Even if one does not exist, someone has to develop it. With two decades of experience, I want to help others. This mindset has provided me with immense customer satisfaction. God has blessed me even during tough times when I had a lot to bear, but as a woman in business, I couldn't afford to have a negative attitude. If you are eager to discover the specific formula to positively transform what you have been doing, then you are in the right place.

In the sales world, many people often quit when they cannot achieve their goals. Let me tell you one thing: quitting is always easier than persevering, but quitting should be the last option. Numerous factors contribute to success, and I am here to help as much as I can. So, what is a vehicle exchange training program, and why do automobile professionals need it?

A vehicle exchange training program is a game changer for salespeople who want to build strong connections with their customers. This program offers your customers a guaranteed trade-in value for their vehicle, often above market value. This not only incentivizes them to upgrade to a new vehicle but also rewards their loyalty to your dealership.

Here's how it works: when a customer is ready to upgrade, you'll inspect their vehicle to determine its condition and reconditioning costs. Then, you'll present them with a trade-in value guaranteed for a set period, usually 12-24 months. This value is typically higher than they would receive on the open market, making it a compelling reason to stay with your dealership.

By offering this program, you'll increase customer satisfaction, drive sales, and boost your bottom line. Plus, it's a great way to differentiate your dealership from the competition and build a loyal customer base. So, start offering your customers a Vehicle Exchange Program today and watch your sales soar! However, this is just a simplified overview of what occurs in this process.

Beginning With the Training Program

Since each dealership faces unique challenges and requirements, there isn't a one-size-fits-all solution. For example, the training might need to address a tendency among salespeople to focus too heavily on price discussions with customers instead of conducting thorough pre-demonstration vehicle inspections and effectively building value. In some cases, the initial training may need to target the sales managers themselves. Even if the sales staff performs adequately, the managers may lack the necessary skills to elevate their team's capabilities. After participating in train-the-trainer workshops, managers often express newfound awareness of their knowledge gaps, demonstrating valuable self-reflection and a willingness to learn. When developing a sales training plan, involving all the managers in the process is crucial. Relying on a single manager to handle all the training can set the organization up for potential issues. Regardless of the manager's expertise as a trainer, any future challenges in the dealership could lead to that individual being unfairly singled out as the scapegoat, so a collective approach is recommended. This ensures that customers receive the Ritz Carlton experience, which means fulfilling their suppressed wishes and needs by providing them with the best service possible. However, to reach that level, we will discuss it in depth in the following segments of this book. Continue reading and be part of this promising journey. By the end of this book, I want to ensure that my readers take away the essence of motivation to taste the fruits of success and maximize their incomes.

Chapter 2: Meet 'n' Greet in Car Sales

A salesperson receives thorough training on how to meet and greet customers. This training teaches them to maintain a positive attitude toward customers, which plays an instrumental role and is the most important aspect of any sale. Consider this simple example: if you visit someone's house and are not greeted warmly, would you go in? Even if you do enter, you might never return. The same principle applies when dealing with customers. From a customer's perspective, they are out to have a seamless and memorable experience. In today's advanced era, where everything is available online, in-person market research shows that customers walking in seek more than just market prices.

Now, think about a situation where a customer has entered your store; it's your duty to provide them with the best experience. What would you do? How would you initiate that interaction and take it from there? You are here to offer your customer a Ritz Carlton-level experience, often regarded as a benchmark for service processes. They aim not only to meet expectations but to exceed them, creating an extraordinary experience. Employees at such establishments are trained to foster unique, memorable, and personal experiences by being responsive to customers' needs and wishes.

Throughout my years of experience, I've often wondered why customers don't simply walk up and express their desires immediately. Wouldn't it make the process easier? Why don't they just say, "We are looking for this specific vehicle and want to buy it. Can you show us, please?" instead of saying, "We are conducting a market survey, driving around to every dealership we can find," or "We have other cars to check out"?

This situation is not unlike deciding to buy the latest model of a phone. Everyone wants the newest and best model, but when they get to the store, they often feel overwhelmed. They admire the phones from a distance but hesitate to approach the sales associate. Why? It's because they don't know what to say or what questions to ask. Remember, most people buy a new phone only every 2–3 years, while sales associates do this every day. Customers may not understand the technical specifications, various plan options, or how to get the best deal. The initial greeting and needs assessment are crucial to the sales process. If the sales associate can engage the customer and understand their specific needs, they have a much better chance of finding the perfect phone and exciting the customer to make the purchase.

Keep in mind that there are millions of dealerships out there, but what will set you apart from your competitors is you. It's like being a concierge; when a person comes for a meet-and-greet, you must have a lights, camera, and action mindset. One important aspect of speaking to a customer is to make them feel as though you are talking to them, not at them. There is a significant difference.

In the world of sales, the initial greeting is akin to an experienced preacher's "amen." It can make or break the entire interaction. Just as a passionate "amen" can captivate a congregation, a genuine, personalized greeting can set the tone for a successful car-buying journey.

Now, imagine a scenario where a new customer walks into your store. A customer enters your showroom like a parishioner entering a place of worship. They are here for guidance, ready to absorb a meaningful experience. Your role as a sales professional is to welcome them with open arms (not literally!), making them feel valued and understood from the very first moment.

Furthermore, it is not enough to recite a scripted greeting. You must connect with the customer on a deeper level, speaking to them as if you have known them for years. They will quickly assess whether they feel a genuine rapport within the first few minutes.

Now you may be wondering: how can this rapport be established in the first place? Well, for starters:

- Begin with a warm, genuine smile, followed by an attentive and conversational demeanor.
- Engage with customers, not at them, and ensure your body language and tone convey a genuine desire to understand their needs and preferences.
- Remember, the customer is the star of the show, and you should be prepared to roll out the red carpet! Greet

them enthusiastically, making their satisfaction your top priority.

- Avoid pressuring customers with any statements that might make them feel uncomfortable.

So, what are the words to use when a customer walks in? There are two types of customers: new and returning. Regardless of which type they are, you should provide them with royal treatment. Here's how to begin the conversation with a new customer:

"Welcome to ABC Motors. My name is ____, and you are? It's a pleasure to meet you, [customer name]." This simple introduction can go a long way in getting the customer started on what they are really looking for.

You can continue the conversation by asking questions such as:

- "Are you looking for something new or pre-owned today?"
- "What other types of vehicles have you been considering?"
- "Great! What did you like about those vehicles?" or "What didn't you like about them?" These questions can help you understand your customer's preferences better.
- "Well, I think I have just the vehicle that could meet your criteria. Let me get you some information on the XYZ car."

Another important aspect that can often be overlooked is ensuring that customers do not feel pressured. To avoid this, you can reassure them with phrases like:

- "Feel free to take your time, ask any questions you may have, and let me know how I can best assist you."
- "If you like what you hear, wonderful! If not, no problem at all."

Though these points may seem simple, they should be applied correctly. A key aspect of the interaction is ensuring the customer feels valued and respected. You don't want them to think that you only care about showing them cars. Ultimately, as salespeople, we all want to sell a vehicle, which can be a challenging task. However, fostering a friendly dialogue makes the process smoother and more open for both parties. Keep in mind that these initial 15-minute questions can help you get to know your customer better.

At this point, you might not be the only salesperson the customer has approached. They may have been looking around and talking to other salespeople. You need to ensure they are providing you with enough information to help sell them a car.

If you've noticed, until the end of the questions mentioned above, there hasn't been any discussion about selling anything. Customers want sufficient information to satisfy their needs before making a decision. Your role is to provide them with the knowledge they require. You already know that the customer is here for a car, that there are competitors out there, and that they have probably spoken to other salespeople. Yet they are still here, answering your questions. This indicates that something has piqued their interest, and they have not walked away. Now, your job is to find out what brought them here, assist them, and begin the selling process. This step is called needs analysis, and you can start this process once you have eased the customer's mind.

Different Meet and Greet in The Vehicle Exchange Program

Now, let's move on to another topic. We have been discussing meeting and greeting new customers. But what about dealing with a customer in the vehicle exchange department? Here, the process is a bit different.

As the manager of the vehicle exchange, I always start by introducing myself and asking the customer how they are doing. This helps set a friendly and personalized tone. You can say *"We appreciate your loyalty and choosing us for service."* Trust me these little words matter.

After that, I make sure to know what customers want. So, I exchange names and do a quick assessment to know them even if it's just for service. I then transition into the key part of the meet and greet: "Quick question for you: if I could give you more than your car is worth, throw in some free extras, and help you save money, would you be interested in potentially upgrading your vehicle today?"

This question may seem a bit direct, but after discussing it well, you can confidently ask this question.

The goal here is to gauge their openness to exploring a vehicle exchange while also emphasizing that the focus is on saving them money and providing a great offer. I avoid using the word "deal," as some customers may be put off by that term.

It's important to remember that service customers are the bread and butter of the dealership. Even if they decline the vehicle exchange offer, it's crucial to make them feel appreciated. You might say, "No problem at all, Mr. and Mrs. Jones. Thank you for choosing us for your service needs. We truly appreciate your business. Please let us know if there is anything else we can do for you."

The way you end the interaction, regardless of their interest in the vehicle exchange, can make a significant difference. Customers want to feel valued, and simply acknowledging their choice to do business with you can go a long way. If the customer declines, let them know you appreciate their decision. Remember, service is a dealership's bread and butter, so you are there to express gratitude, whether the answer is yes or no.

As a closing note, you can say, "Mr./Ms. ABC, thank you for choosing us. We truly appreciate you. If there's anything we can do for you in the future, please let us know."

This approach helps cultivate loyalty and increases the likelihood that they will return. Moreover, when people feel appreciated and valued, they are more likely to come back. This guide is designed to enhance your knowledge with each chapter. If you follow these instructions carefully, there's a very low chance you will feel discouraged. The key is to keep up with the guide and work smartly.

Benefits of the vehicle exchange program:

The vehicle exchange program allows the dealership to acquire used cars from customers who are trading in or upgrading their vehicles. These acquired vehicles become part of the dealership's used car inventory. Since these vehicles were serviced at the dealership previously, they come with service records, which is valuable information for potential buyers. This process helps the dealership build its used car inventory without having to purchase vehicles at auctions. It's beneficial because the dealership gets used cars with known service histories, which can be more appealing to customers and potentially easier to sell.

Key Takeaways from This Chapter

- The meet and greet is the most important part of a sale. Greet customers warmly and make them feel welcome.
- There are two types of customers: new customers and service customers. The meet and greet process is slightly different for each.

- For service customers, ask if you could offer them more for their trade-ins and upgrades to encourage consideration of a new vehicle.
- Even if a service customer declines an upgrade, always thank them sincerely for their business. Value the relationship.

Chapter 3: Needs Analysis

When it comes to the needs analysis of a car buyer, there are crucial points for a salesperson to keep in mind to facilitate the process for both parties. As discussed in the previous chapter, which served as an introductory guide on "Meet and Greet," we now move on to the next important step, which is also the roadmap to the sale.

A salesperson must have the right mindset and approach. The right mindset isn't just about commanding the room and capturing the customer's full attention; it's about owning the entire building while you serve. It also involves confidence and the way you carry yourself.

A good salesperson is genuinely interested in understanding the customer's needs and requirements. Unfortunately, there is often a negative perception of salespeople. Many believe that salespeople are merely trying to convince customers to pay high prices for products. However, the reality of sales is quite the opposite. In all my years of experience, that has never been the case. If it were, I might have switched careers long ago.

One thing is clear: customers are not fools. The idea that a salesperson can trick someone into buying at a higher price is as absurd as taking a pill to induce frustration and headaches. A salesperson's job is to determine why a customer is at their doorstep and what was on their mind when they decided to come in. As a salesperson, I earn my commission by successfully selling a car, so why wouldn't I make an effort to meet the customer's needs?

This brings us to needs analysis, which serves as your compass and roadmap to the sale. This analysis takes time, and there's no need to rush! Taking the time to thoroughly understand the customer's situation, preferences, and pain points is essential. Rushing through this process can lead to missed opportunities and wasted efforts. As I often emphasize, "Anything you don't get right in the needs analysis will leave you working hard rather than smart."

The process begins with gathering the necessary information. In sales, this is known as the SPIN selling method, which stands for Situation, Problem, Implication, and Need Pay-off. There are four types of questions based on these categories, all of which are proven techniques used by many experts.

This method helps uncover customers' pain points by highlighting the consequences of their problems and the benefits of your solutions as a salesperson. It also builds rapport, trust, and credibility with customers, as it reflects empathy and genuine interest.

When it comes to a vehicle exchange, the process starts similarly with gathering necessary information. First, approach the customer in the service department and obtain the repair order (RO) that contains their name, address, and telephone number. This information can then be entered into your company's customer relationship management (CRM) system to determine if the customer has purchased from your dealership before.

If the customer is a repeat buyer, you have a significant advantage. By accessing the "back screen" in your CRM system, you can gain valuable insights into their previous purchases, allowing you to personalize your approach and demonstrate your appreciation for their loyalty. This level of knowledge will help the customer feel more comfortable and engaged throughout the sales process.

However, not every business has a robust CRM system. In such cases, the salesperson must be resourceful and proactive. Even if the customer's information is recorded manually or in a simple system, reviewing the details of their previous deal is crucial before engaging with them. Approaching a vehicle exchange situation "blindly" can harm the sales process.

The key is to make the whole experience pleasant for the customer. I often mention the Ritz Carlton experience because the main goal is to provide luxury with civility and elegance. Sometimes, luxury is not everything; how you handle customers and take care of their needs is what truly matters.

Get your customers seated and let them know that your presence is meant to make things easier, not to confuse them. Once seated, review their vehicle information on the screen. In the meantime, offer them something to drink. The vehicle information will tell you when they bought it, what they paid, mileage, interest rate, and loan term—very handy information indeed! I wouldn't recommend vehicle exchanges to new employees, as seasoned employees can carry out this task more efficiently, and to excel in sales, experience is crucial.

The screen before you is your success strategy. First, check the current interest rate. Even if it's only slightly better, assure them you can secure a lower one. Then, discuss upgrading perks like an extended warranty if they trade in. Warranties provide peace of mind by covering repairs.

The next crucial step is reviewing costs. Trading up means lower maintenance and ownership costs down the line compared to keeping an older vehicle. Once you've reviewed everything, ask what colors and options they like best that they didn't have before. Then, you can tell them you have the perfect vehicle in mind! The next step is to ask them to wait a few minutes while you pull up their preferred vehicle.

At this point, you are facilitating a test drive. This applies specifically to a vehicle exchange situation, but if a customer walks in without the intention of exchanging a vehicle, you, as a salesperson, need to work smart. In this case, you won't have any prior information that could help make the process smoother. However, being resourceful will allow you to quickly get to the core of the customer's needs. Remember, Rome wasn't built in a day, so it takes time to create great things.

Here, you should ask rapid-fire questions instead of engaging in a lengthy conversation where you listen and then provide information. If you encounter resistance, don't panic. That's where your managers come in handy. We'll refer to them as EMAs—Emergency Manager Assistants.

Reaching out for help doesn't mean you've failed. In fact, it shows intelligence to tap into their experience when needed. Nobody knows everything in their first weeks. I certainly didn't! EMAs are well-compensated because they can smooth over any rough patches. Remember, no one starts out knowing how to do this job. We all begin as beginners. Leaning on managers is how you learn the ropes without risking a sale. When they come over, just listen—don't jump in. Absorb what you can so that next time, you can handle it on your own. The more you can do independently, the quicker you'll advance, just like the EMAs.

For instance, Maria was working with José on a new vehicle purchase. During the needs analysis, José seemed hesitant, and his body language conveyed discomfort. Remembering her training, Maria said, "Let me check a few things with my manager. I'll be right back." She asked José to have a seat and then pulled Brandon, her manager, aside to explain the situation before he approached José.

In another scenario, Luis was meeting with Tina but got stumped when she asked about financing options for buyers with less-than-perfect credit. Rather than guess, Luis said, "I don't have all the details on that program, but my manager Juan is an expert on financing. Let me have him come over so you get the right information." He asked Tina to stay seated while he fetched Juan.

In both cases, the salespeople protected the sale by not leaving the customer waiting or providing misinformation. Tapping into their manager's expertise helped improve the customer experience. The key is to keep potential buyers comfortable while getting the assistance needed to move the sale forward.

Another way to look at it is that when you are at the desk with customers, you are building credibility and trust. If you say something incorrectly, it might not reflect well on you. As a car salesperson, you cannot afford to have a bad reputation. Your role is not only to be confident but also to be unique and memorable. Consider what makes you different from other car sellers. What do you offer that others don't? Once you help the customer let their guard down, you will not only sell a car but also gain a new friend. The chances of a satisfied customer returning are always high, which is the ultimate goal.

Moreover, once connections are formed, customers will gladly spread your name like sweet songbirds sharing notes on a great find. As the saying goes, the best type of advertising is word of mouth.

Last but not least, customers will test your knowledge, so always do your homework. Listen carefully to their hopes for their new vehicle. Keep your responses personalized, never preachy, and focus on their joy rather than your profit. Customers can sense empty flattery, but genuine warmth turns strangers into allies.

As the Siebel ad says, "Good service is good business."

This is a sample form for Needs Analysis

*Salesperson:*____________________*Date:*____________
Customer #: ____________________

*What model are you interested in?*______________

Stock #: ___________________

What is most important to you?

A. ____________________/______________________
B. ____________________/______________________
C. ____________________/______________________
D. ____________________/______________________

Tell us about your car.

Will you be adding or replacing?

____

Year: ___________________*Make:* ____________________
Model: ____________________

What made you choose this vehicle?

____

What did you like the most?

________________________/_______________________

Price of the present vehicle? ________

Current Payment? _______*Initial investment?* ________

Would you like a fair market appraisal?

Yes ________No__________

Who will be the primary driver?________________________

How many others? __________

How many miles do you drive a year? ________

How long do you keep your vehicle? ________

Would you like to consider alternative options?

Yes _____No _____

What other than a [abc car] interests you?

____

Have you driven? Yes/ No, Found interesting?

____

How would you like us to present pricing?

Finance – Lease options- Cash price

If Payment option:

New Monthly Budget: ___________

Cash investment: ____________________________

Name:_________________________

Address: ____

City:____

State: ________Zip: _________

Work: ________________________Home: _______________
Cell: ________________________

E-mail:

Source:________________________ ☐W/I ☐P/U ☐ Internet

Estimated pay off: ______________________Name of Lender: ____________________________

Sales Manager: _________________________

Comments

____

____

____

____

When Figures are agreeable and affordable, how soon would you like to start enjoying your new vehicle,
today________or tomorrow _______?

How to answer a lead or a phone call regarding a vehicle?

When answering a phone call about a vehicle, it is crucial to remember that this is the first point of contact between the dealership and the customer. Often, multiple dealerships may receive the same lead, so it's important to stand out. Personalizing communication is key, so rather than using generic templates, the representatives should introduce themselves warmly, expressing gratitude for the customer's interest in a specific vehicle.

You say, " My name is [your name]. Thank you for your interest in [XYZ vehicle]. I look forward to earning your business and providing outstanding service."

When handling inquiries, the goal should be to set an appointment rather than negotiate over the phone. Even if the customer is asking for the price of a certain vehicle, it's important to limit the information shared to avoid a bidding war. Create urgency by suggesting the vehicle is in high demand. Phrasing like, "Can you come in today or tomorrow?" can help secure an appointment.

If a customer expresses concern about pricing, you can reassure them, saying, "Our dealership has very deep pockets. The hardest part is ensuring this is the right vehicle for you." They should then redirect the conversation back to schedule a visit.

But if the caller keeps reiterating regarding price, then what?

Well, it's simple. You let them know and feel that money is the latter part. What matters is their presence, as that will create the opportunity for both parties to earn the business together.

Once an appointment is set, it's important to confirm it in the CRM system to protect the deal. Finally, the representative should send a text with their business card, including their contact information, to ascertain that the customer knows who to reach out to if they need assistance before their visit.

In the end, don't get caught up in the distractions. What I meant by “distractions” is that when you gather with a few colleagues, start chatting and suddenly realize the day has slipped away. Remember that your primary focus in the dealership should be on the phone, whether you’re dialing for appointments, sending emails, or greeting customers. Engaging in casual conversations can be tempting, but those moments won't help you meet your goals or pay your bills. So, stay focused on what truly matters.

Key Takeaways from This Chapter

- Leverage customer relationship management (CRM) systems to access past purchase information, especially for repeat customers, allowing for a personalized sales approach.
- Create a pleasant atmosphere for customers and ensure they understand that your goal is to assist them, not to confuse them.
- Don’t hesitate to seek assistance from more experienced colleagues when faced with customer questions or concerns; this demonstrates wisdom and fosters a better customer experience.
- A salesperson must maintain a good reputation by providing accurate information and building trust, which leads to repeat business and referrals.

- Always personalize interactions based on customer preferences and maintain a warm approach to turn potential buyers into loyal customers.
- Satisfied customers are likely to recommend you to others, making word-of-mouth referrals a powerful marketing tool.
- Keep an extra effort on making phone calls and keep up with the appointment.

Chapter 4: Test Drive

Why does a salesperson prioritize test drives? Experienced salespeople often assert that the test drive itself can be a key factor in selling cars. Once the test drive is complete, the most common obstacle customers face is typically the price of the vehicle.

It's important to recognize that the purpose of the test drive is not to showcase the features and benefits of a car, as that should have already been covered during the initial walkaround earlier in the sales process. At this stage, the customer you're working with has likely done extensive online research on the vehicles they're interested in, so you don't need to provide that information unless they specifically ask for it. The primary reason for a test drive is to allow the customer to envision themselves driving a particular vehicle in the long term.

When a customer experiences the acceleration and maneuverability of a vehicle firsthand, an emotional connection is formed. While this may seem unusual or unconvincing, many people do indeed develop a sense of emotional attachment to their vehicles. This connection can begin to take shape during the test drive.

Although the customer may not verbalize all of their questions during the test drive, you can assume they are considering various aspects internally, such as whether the vehicle will be suitable for long family road trips, how it will perform in snowy winter conditions, and if it will fit in their garage. These are just a few examples of the types of questions the customer is likely pondering before making their final purchase decision.

If you want to go the extra mile, many salespeople display vehicle information on a computer screen, similar to watching a video, to give the customer more details about the car they're interested in. This can really enhance the sales experience.

It's important to never have the customer accompany you to retrieve the vehicle. Instead, make them comfortable while you prepare the car. This allows you to adjust the temperature to their preference, whether it needs to be cooled or heated, depending on the weather.

Additionally, it's a good idea to have calm, unobtrusive music playing, such as classical or elevator music. This helps create a relaxed atmosphere for the test drive, but ensure it is not too loud, as that could make the experience unpleasant for the customer. Avoid potentially jarring music choices; the goal is to help them focus on the driving experience itself. Elevator music is a safe choice that won't offend anyone. Your aim is to make the customer feel relaxed and comfortable.

Things to Take Care of Before the Test Drive

Before the customer arrives, make sure to warm up the car and have classical or elevator music playing to set the right mood. Keep some microfiber cloths handy, too; you can quickly wipe down the interior to make it look its best. Paying attention to these small details is important.

When the customer shows up, start the walkthrough from the passenger side door. Move methodically, going from the hood to the back seat and trunk, and end at the driver's side door. Once you reach the driver's door, invite the customer to get comfortable. Have them put on their seatbelt and adjust the mirrors and seat. Don't just ask if they want to test drive; guide them through the step-by-step process.

The key is to create a smooth, professional experience that puts the customer at ease. Never overlook small details that might seem insignificant to many; a true salesperson knows that music and interior cleaning can make a big difference.

Before anything else, when you conduct the initial needs analysis with the customer, it's crucial to obtain a copy of their driver's license. Do not proceed with a test drive without first obtaining this copy. Once you have it, keep that copy securely on your desk.

There are compliance reasons for maintaining a copy of the customer's license. It's important to keep your desk locked at all times in case there is ever an audit. Additionally, you should leave a copy of the license with your manager before going out on the test drive.

Informing your manager about the test drive is a matter of safety protocol. Unfortunately, there have been instances where something unexpected has happened during a test drive, and without anyone knowing the customer's identity or whereabouts, it becomes very difficult to respond effectively. By leaving a copy of the license with your manager, you ensure there is a record and someone who can be notified in an emergency.

As a salesperson looking to close a deal, you must take care of these important steps. This protects both you and the customer and aligns with essential compliance requirements. By addressing these aspects upfront, the entire process can proceed smoothly.

Planning A Route for The Test Drive

When taking the customer on a test drive, you should have a designated route planned out ahead of time. The general guideline is to avoid making left-hand turns during the test drive; instead, stick to right-hand turns only.

You also want to avoid taking the customer onto the highway unless they specifically request it. Keep the test drive short, ideally around 5-10 minutes, in the local area near the dealership.

Once you've completed the test drive, the key question to ask the customer is: "Mr./Ms. XYZ, do you like this car well enough to own it today? If we can make the numbers agreeable, do you like it enough to own it today?" This is a question you should ask today, not tomorrow.

Regardless of their initial response, whether it's "I think so" or something else, instruct them to follow you back to your desk to discuss the numbers and paperwork.

It's also imperative that the customer drives the vehicle during the test drive. If they say they don't feel like driving, you should insist that they at least drive it around the parking lot. Ninety-nine percent of the time, if they don't drive the car, they won't end up buying it. So, you must get them behind the wheel.

If you follow this formula, you will ensure a smooth and productive test drive experience.

Important Rules to Keep in Mind

1. **The customer must drive the vehicle during the test drive.** This is non-negotiable. If the customer resists driving, pause and say, "Let me get a manager to help with this." Then, go and get a manager to assist in getting the customer behind the wheel.
2. **Thoroughly demonstrate all features and functions.** Show the customer features like Apple CarPlay, the navigation system, and all safety features. The goal is to engage the customer emotionally and make them excited about the car.
3. **Conduct the walkaround and feature demonstration before the test drive.** This ensures the customer is already familiar with the car when you head out on the road.

4. **Never leave the car keys unattended after the test drive.** Always keep the keys with you. If you leave them on the desk, someone could swap them out and steal the vehicle. Maintaining full control of the keys is critical.

Remember, contrary to the common stereotype, the most successful salespeople are not pushy or aggressive. Instead, they are genuine, caring, and attentive in their approach. Building genuine rapport and trust with customers is key to being an effective salesperson. Just be yourself as you cultivate an authentic relationship with the customer. By focusing on what the customer values, you create an experience that leaves them feeling genuinely cared for, not pressured, which is the foundation for building long-term loyalty and generating recurring business.

Key Takeaways from This Chapter

- It's not about showcasing features, which should have been covered earlier, but allowing customers to envision themselves driving the car.
- To enhance the experience, ensure the car is warmed up, play calm music, and keep the interior clean.
- Always obtain a copy of the customer's driver's license for compliance and safety reasons and inform your manager before the test drive.
- Plan a route that avoids left-hand turns and highways, keeping it short and local.

- Ensure you demonstrate all features before the test drive and keep the keys secure afterward.
- Lastly, successful salespeople build genuine relationships with customers, focusing on their needs and creating a comfortable, caring environment.

Chapter 5: Negotiations

Negotiation can be challenging yet rewarding in the automobile industry. Mastering this essential skill as a seller is crucial for achieving goals and avoiding difficulties in the process. Negotiations determine whether a customer will merely browse or become a lifelong client. In this chapter, we will explore the delicate balance between urgency and pressure and how to navigate the negotiation process with finesse.

The first and foremost aspect is to be persuasive but in a positive way. Your job is to assure the customer that you are here to help, making things easier for both of you. It's important to remember that you don't want to pressure them, as this can backfire and cost you a loyal customer or even the entire deal. The key is to strike a balance between urgency and pressure.

As you present a deal that creates a sense of urgency, ensure that there is no pressure to decide immediately. Encourage the customer to share their thoughts and feelings—if they like what they hear, great! If not, that's okay too.

The next step is to explain the process, especially for a new customer. When you return with a "pencil" (a preliminary offer) from your manager, be transparent about the process. Explain to your customer that this is a normal part of the negotiation, and if they don't like what they see, that's perfectly fine. Approach the discussion with a professional and direct tone, much like an attorney, and walk them through the numbers. Don't be intimidated by the figures—your customer is the one who will be paying, not you.

The goal is to create a positive environment, which is crucial. A stress-free experience benefits both parties. Clear communication builds rapport and trust, so using the right communication style should never be overlooked.

But what do you do when you don't like the offer you just made? The initial offer is just that—an initial offer. If the customer doesn't like what they see, don't fret. This is an opportunity to understand their needs and concerns more deeply. Take the time to listen carefully to what they have to say and address each point with empathy and understanding.

For example, if your customer says, "That's just not going to work for me," respond with, "I understand, Mr./Ms. XYZ. Please tell me more about what's not working for you, and I'll do my best to find a solution that better fits your needs."

Here, you must present the best options for the customer's benefit, which will also benefit you. Moreover, the key to successful negotiation is ensuring that the customer sees the value in the deal. They're unlikely to move forward if they don't perceive a clear benefit. That's why it's crucial to spend more time listening than talking during this phase.

The old saying, "The first one to speak loses," holds true here. Let your customer guide the conversation and use this time to understand their priorities and concerns. Only then can you craft a proposal that addresses their needs and leaves them feeling satisfied.

If issues arise, such as the customer feeling they aren't getting enough for their trade-in, don't simply deny their claim. Instead, take them to the vehicle and walk them through the details, pointing out any imperfections or factors influencing the offer. After that, find a middle ground. Adjusting the trade-in value in small increments, such as $100 at a time, allows you to reach an agreement without making drastic concessions.

Additionally, you must be well aware of the laws in your state. For example, in Georgia, customers only pay taxes on the difference if they have a trade-in. Doing your research and understanding these nuances can help you tailor your approach and find a solution that works for everyone. As you guide customers through the negotiation process, ensure they don't feel overwhelmed.

As they say in negotiation, if they give you a commitment, make sure you write it down. Although it sounds simple, doing so demonstrates professionalism and ensures that any agreements made are clearly documented and understood by both parties. When you present the written commitment to the customer, say, "Mr./Ms. Name], let's go ahead and jot this down so we both have a clear record of what we've discussed. This shows that I'm serious about making this work for you."

Before you dive into the numbers, take a moment to confirm essential details by asking the customer, "Is this going to be titled in your name? And is this the address we have on file?" Then carefully go over the vehicle information, trade-in details, and the customer's personal information to stage a smooth, transparent negotiation process.

When reviewing the numbers, approach the discussion with a methodical yet conversational pace. Avoid rushing through the figures; present them clearly and numerically. If the customer has any questions, be sure to address them promptly.

As you conclude the number review, use this simple but powerful phrase: "Mr./Ms. Name], all I need is your signature here, and we'll get you all set up for delivery. Does this work for you?"

Keep in mind that not all negotiations will go smoothly. Sometimes, you will hear "no" as a response, but remember that a "no" from the customer is not the end of the road. In fact, it's an opportunity to showcase your negotiation skills and turn the tide in your favor. As one of my mentors wisely said, "Anybody can take an order, but not everyone can sell a car and show its value." After all, customers don't come to a dealership just to browse; they're here to buy a car. It's up to you to guide them through the negotiation process, uncover their true needs, and present a deal that they simply can't refuse.

Now, if the customer says no during the negotiation, there are usually three main reasons: the price, the monthly payments, or the need to discuss it with their spouse. For the price, let the customer know that you've done a thorough research and that this is one of the best prices in the area. This demonstrates that you're being upfront and transparent.

Regarding the payments, always remember that the down payment affects the monthly cost. Ask the customer how much they can put down. If it's not enough, see if you can approve them for a longer term to lower the monthly amount.

If they say they need to talk to their spouse, that's totally understandable. Suggest getting the spouse on a video call right then, so you can all discuss it together. This shows you're flexible and want to accommodate their needs. If they can't get on a video call at that moment, get permission from your manager to take the customer for a test drive in the car.

You'll need to ensure you have a copy of their driver's license and insurance info first. This way, you can bring the car directly to the spouse so they can see it and discuss it together. You have a couple of options here: either get them on a video call or accompany the customer to show the car to their significant other. One of those two actions needs to happen because you don't want to just send the customer back out on their own.

If you do that, all the work you've put in so far will be for nothing. They'll probably just go look at cars somewhere else. And no one enjoys the car-buying process, right? So, if you can provide them with an amazing experience and show them the true value of the car, they're much more likely to buy it from you.

But if they don't believe in you or feel that connection, they won't. As I mentioned at the start, people buy from people they like—about 80-90% of the time. The other 10% is just knowledge. If they like you, they'll buy from you.

We understand that buying a car is not a small or everyday decision, and most people visit at least three dealerships before making up their minds. That's why it's so important for you, as the salesperson, to be a closer. When a customer walks in and is ready to buy, you need to ensure the experience is great and sell them that car!

The key (as discussed previously) is to listen more than you talk. Go through your needs analysis with the customer and focus on understanding what they are looking for. If you do that, I guarantee you'll successfully sell them the car.

Another sticking point can be trade-ins. If a customer is interested in trading in their vehicle, do a full walk-around with them and point out any issues with their current car. In the automotive sales business, this walk is called a trade walk. This gives you an opportunity to gain the customer's trust and be a bit creative as you help them look at the insides of the car or get them seated in the driver's seat.

People often think their trade is worth more than it actually is, so managing that expectation is important. Even if the customer says no, you may never see them again. So, don't be afraid to be direct while also maintaining control of the situation. If they want the deal, they'll take it from you. And not only will they buy from you, but they'll also tell their family and friends.

However, if you find that you are losing deals more often than not, you need to go back to the basics. The good thing is that this book comes with a support system for everyone who gets it. So, if you're struggling, just email customer support, and we can work through it together.

The car business is very lucrative, but you have to be the best of the best. That starts with believing in yourself. Nobody is going to believe in you more than you believe in yourself. As a salesperson, you must speak confidently, stand tall, and truly believe in what you're saying and how you present it. If you do that, the rest will fall into place.

The key points here apply to the car business and any sales industry—real estate, vacuum cleaners, whatever it may be. At the end of the day, it's all about the product. But more importantly, it's about the person selling that product.

People buy from people they like. If they like you, they'll buy from you. If they don't, they won't. So, before you even get to the negotiating table, offer them something to drink and make them feel comfortable. The first impression of you and your business will set the tone for the entire interaction. If you can get them to relax and feel at home, they are more likely to open up, trust you, and ultimately want to do business with you.

It's the small gestures that can make a big difference. Extending the same hospitality, you'd show a guest in your own home goes a long way. It makes the customer feel valued, respected, and eager to continue the conversation. That kind of positive experience doesn't just lead to a sale;

it can turn a customer into a loyal brand advocate who raves about you to everyone they know. Always keep that customer-first mentality, and the rest will follow.

Key Takeaways from This Chapter

- Be persuasive but avoid pressure; create a sense of urgency without overwhelming the customer.
- Explain the negotiation process transparently, ensuring they understand it's normal to discuss offers.
- Listen carefully to customer concerns and present solutions that highlight the value of the deal.
- Take a methodical approach to presenting figures, addressing questions promptly.
- If faced with a "no," identify the reason—price, payments, or need to consult a spouse—and respond accordingly.
- Confidence is key; believe in yourself and your product.
- Always prioritize the customer's needs for long-term success.

Chapter 6: Delivery Surveys

As the years have passed, the delivery process of cars has changed drastically. Salespeople no longer just toss you the keys and wish you well; there's a comprehensive process in place known as the delivery process. This process holds significant weight, as it is often time-consuming and closely linked to customer satisfaction.

Once the deal is sealed and all financial checks have been approved, the next step is to deliver the vehicle. This delivery is connected to a survey, and where there is a survey, there is a monetary value attached to it. Therefore, during this crucial phase of the sale, it is essential to slow down the pace. Attention to detail becomes paramount, ensuring that every box is checked.

I take the time to ensure the customer is well-prepared for the handover experience. While they engage with the business manager in finance, I make it a point to set the stage for their vehicle introduction. This involves creating a welcoming environment by organizing my workspace, laying out the owner's manual and other relevant materials, and carefully reviewing each document together.

I believe it is imperative not to simply hand over the owner's manual in a rushed manner, as this could give the impression of a transactional exchange. Instead, I use this moment to explore the finer details, slow down, and express genuine gratitude for their decision to choose our dealership for their vehicle purchase. I often relate the owner's manual to the “bible” of their car, highlighting its significance in maximizing their driving experience.

For those who prefer a more concise approach, I guide them to the QR code on the back cover as an alternative source of information. Once scanned, this QR code directs them straight to the online guide. While writing this guidebook, I realized there is a gap in automotive guidance. Even with the vast information available online, precise guidance is indeed a blessing, as it saves customers from having to search endlessly.

As a salesperson, don’t assume that the customer knows everything. Your job is to ensure that the customer understands their vehicle well before they hit the road.

The Warranty Book

Now, let’s discuss another essential item to cover: the warranty book. When you reach the first page of the warranty, it’s good to go through it together and quickly review the details. Additionally, within each owner’s manual laid out on the desk, you will typically find this information.

Let me share what I do. I like to capture a picture of this setup to provide a visual reference for the customer. If you follow this method, you will have a handy guide for organizing your materials. There are also a couple of federal forms that can be handed over to the customer for review.

At this point, a valuable resource is the quick reference guide. This guide is placed right after the owner’s manual and serves as a convenient tool for quick information retrieval. For example, if you can't find something in the extensive owner's manual, you can turn to the quick reference guide for a more concise answer.

Most manufacturers include complimentary roadside assistance for customers. It's a small but important detail that I always make sure to highlight. I recommend storing the roadside assistance number in the customer's phone for easy access. I say, "Mr. and Mrs. XYZ, please allow me to provide you with the contact details for roadside assistance. I'd rather you have it and not need it than need it and not have it." This is when you will input the roadside assistance number into their phone. Remember, if you do not program that number into your customer's phone, you are doing them a disservice.

Regarding the owner's manual, don't forget to slip a few handy cards into the designated slot. These little touches make a big difference, much like adding seasoning to a dish to enhance its flavor.

Being Thoughtful About the Whole Process

One important aspect of this process—and I believe it is just as crucial as all the other steps—is being thoughtful. Customers truly appreciate thoughtful gestures and gifts. It's like planting seeds of kindness that bloom into goodwill. I often stop by the dollar store to pick up gift bags and select items for both men and women. Putting the owner's manual in a gift bag and placing it on a brand-new seat adds a special touch that customers love.

I also like to grab some microfiber cloths from Costco to give to each customer. Just as a gentle touch can clean a delicate surface, these cloths help keep the car screen spotless. Keep in mind that personal touches leave a lasting impression, like adding a big red bow to the car or asking if there's a special occasion to celebrate during the delivery. Personalizing the experience creates a memorable moment that customers will cherish, making the overall experience unforgettable.

The Lengthy Paperwork with The Customer

Now, this is the point where a buyer might think that the process is over. However, it isn't. The delivery process consumes a significant amount of time due to the paperwork involved. While you have successfully sold a car and ensured all the steps are taken in a timely manner, the after-service is equally important. You should call the customer a few days later to check on their experience with the new vehicle.

Since buying or exchanging a vehicle requires many steps, you can reassure the customer that you are here for them if they ever forget something. Even if they have the manual, the most important thing is to familiarize the customer with their new car. Let them know they can always come back or call if they need assistance.

As I mentioned earlier, the delivery process can be time-consuming, including learning everything about the vehicle from A to Z. One way to make a positive impression is by offering the customer a snack. Just like top universities provide excellent service, asking if they're hungry demonstrates your attention to detail. Different people have different preferences, and most dealerships have a Chick-fil-A nearby. If not, suggesting ordering a pizza can also be a nice touch. It's the small gestures that matter, creating a welcoming atmosphere. This is a point I've highlighted in previous chapters as well.

While many may decline the snack offer, some customers appreciate the gesture. In some instances, you might find yourself ordering a pizza or picking up Chick-fil-A for customers—whatever it takes to ensure their satisfaction. The goal is not just to create a one-time customer but to build a lifelong relationship. If I were a customer and someone treated me well, I would definitely return to them.

It is also vital to remind the customer to clear out their previous vehicles, ensuring no personal information is left behind. Don't forget to remove the license plate and return it to them to prevent any potential issues in the future. This shows your care and commitment to customer satisfaction.

One thing worth mentioning is the importance of properly attaching the tag to the car. Show it to the customer and let them know that in most states, they will have their spot before the expiration date. Every state has different rules, so make sure to go through the tag and paperwork, then finalize your deal and have a current insurance card ready. If it's a weekday and they are open, switch the insurance over while waiting for the financing process.

If it's too overwhelming, you can have the customer do it later. But if they are younger and ready to meet with the finance manager, go ahead and have them take care of it. If they are older, be patient and don't rush them. It's always good to make things easier for them by providing a copy of the paperwork as well. In all these steps, prioritizing customer care is key to building strong relationships and fostering loyalty.

Key Takeaways from This Chapter

- After finalizing the deal, take time to ensure a thorough handover experience.
- Organize materials and review documents together with the client, emphasizing the owner's manual as a vital resource.
- Highlight important features like the warranty, roadside assistance, and quick reference guides. Personal touches, such as gift bags and microfiber cloths, enhance the experience and leave lasting impressions.
- Follow up a few days later to check on the customer's satisfaction and remind them they can reach out for help.
- Ensure customers clean out their trade-in vehicles, return license plates, and properly attach new tags.

Chapter 7: Follow-up and Referrals

On the journey of post-sale, the next step is a follow-up, which allows you to uncover opportunities to strengthen your bond with the customer and pave the way for smoother interactions. Let's look at the bigger picture: a dealership's ability to follow up with buyers makes a significant difference. Along with a follow-up plan, a dealership should also include strategies to engage buyers.

It is exciting to reach out to your customer the day after a sale and ask them about their experience with their new car or if they have had any trouble operating its features. It's understandable if they are having difficulty understanding everything; let them know you are here to help. You might wonder how a buyer can still face issues after going through the delivery process, surveys, and test drives. Well, buying a vehicle can be overwhelming, especially for someone who is older or purchasing a car for the very first time.

If a situation like this arises, here's what I prefer to do: I usually invite them over for a refresher course. If they can't come in, I grab a light vehicle and video call them With this advanced use of technology, I can go over everything as if the buyer were in front of me. This is one effective way to connect with the buyer.

You can also phone them, text them, or email them—these are all effective follow-up tools. Communication plays a starring role in sales success. By this point, you have both navigated the buying phase and built a relationship.

In the sales industry, a text or an email is a non-intrusive and budget-friendly way to reach customers. This method allows them to reply at their convenience. Moreover, I have learned that customizing the message for each customer can go a long way in making them feel appreciated.

It is the after-sales service that fosters customer loyalty and generates value. Your goal is to keep the customer returning to you, not to annoy them with unnecessary visits. When speaking with the customer, emphasize that your focus is not just on the sale but also on providing top-notch service afterward.

Let them know that your dealership is dedicated to excellence. When making that follow-up call, be sure to mention the upcoming survey to prepare them. Maintaining this approach consistently is key.

Now is the time to shine by highlighting the importance of Google reviews. Imagine someone searching for your dealership online and seeing all those glowing reviews. Who do you think they'll turn to for help? That's right; they'll be looking for you. Boosting your Google reviews not only benefits your future business but also elevates the dealership's reputation.

Here's what you must do: seize the opportunity to request a review while customers are waiting to finalize their finances or suggest they leave one once they're back home. Remember, securing those Google reviews is important for you. At the right time and without being pushy, you can ask them to leave a review for your dealership.

What to do in follow-up?

Apart from asking customers to review your services on Google and inquiring about their car, what else is there to do? Well, there's one small but impactful thing you can do: send your buyer a "thank you" card along with a couple of your business cards that also include your phone number. Why include your personal phone number in addition to the official one? One reason is that it allows them to reach out to you directly without going through someone else.

After that, follow up on day five and then again on day 10. During this call, ensure they have completed the survey. You can prepare them beforehand to make filling out the survey form easier.

This is also a good time to ask for referrals, but make sure to do it when the customer is satisfied with your services. Let them know they have your number, and if anyone in their family or among their friends needs a car, they should tell them about your dealership.

According to statistics provided by Nielsen, people are four times more likely to buy when referred by a friend or family member. Therefore, when requesting a referral, approach it with humility. You might say, "Mr./Ms. Customer], I would appreciate your help in expanding our business by referring others who might be looking for a car right now or in the near future."

Additionally, you can mention the referral by name, with the permission of your loyal and happy buyers. Explain how you have helped them—from choosing a car to sealing the perfect deal that met their needs.

In the end, always show gratitude for the referral by saying thank you or through thoughtful gifts that reflect your client's personality. Since you have been working with them, don't forget to do your homework on their hobbies; this type of personal touch works wonders. This gesture not only shows your appreciation for their referrals but also motivates them to refer you again.

Always remember the impact of going the extra mile in customer service. Rather than directly requesting referrals from your clients, consider suggesting if they would be open to showcasing your work in a visible place for others to see. This approach allows potential new clients to see real-life examples of your services without putting pressure on your current clients.

Key Takeaways from This Chapter

Effective follow-up after a sale is crucial for building customer relationships and enhancing satisfaction.

Engage with customers the day after their purchase to check on their experience and address any confusion about their vehicle's features.

Focus on providing excellent after-sales service to foster loyalty.

Send a thank-you card with your contact information and follow up again after several days to ensure satisfaction and prompt them to fill out surveys.

Request referrals when customers are happy, emphasizing the value of personal recommendations.

Show gratitude for referrals with thoughtful gifts or gestures, reinforcing the relationship and encouraging future referrals.

Always aim to go the extra mile in customer service to create a positive impression.

Chapter 8: Pandora Box Questions

This chapter is dedicated to the responses we often receive from customers who walk in. I believe these are the most common, which is why I am including this chapter. With years of experience, I have dealt with many customers, and in many cases, their questions and responses were similar.

Each experience with buyers and customers is different. I assure you, it is not that hard to determine who is here to buy and who is just passing by. A list of a few questions at the start will set the tone for the entire customer-salesperson conversation.

However, a good salesperson knows how to engage a customer by understanding them well. Anyone who walks into the showroom has something building up in their mind. While we have discussed in detail how to understand your potential customers and what to do when presenting them with the best deals, you may encounter objections such as:

- ***"It's too much."***
- ***"I have to speak with my significant other."***
- ***"I don't make quick decisions; I want to shop around."***
- ***"I need to talk to my bank."***
- ***"I don't like the color."***
- ***"My car is paid off."***

What should you do then? What should your response be? Let's start with the first one:

"It's too much." If a customer says this, it is one of the most common rejections a salesperson can experience. In this case, take a moment to inquire why they feel that way.

At this point, it is crucial to listen to the customer's concerns. For instance, if they mention seeing a lower price elsewhere, assure them that your dealership conducts thorough research within a wide radius to ensure competitive pricing.

Let them know that your team doesn't just sell cars; they meticulously inspect and prepare each vehicle. Providing this reassurance will give them peace of mind, knowing they're getting a top-quality car. This approach serves as an effective initial response to such concerns.

If the customer says,

"I need to speak to my significant other." In such cases, it's crucial to handle the situation tactfully. After addressing their concern, suggest to Mr. or Ms. Z that they involve their spouse in the decision-making process. You can propose options like calling their spouse, arranging a video call to showcase the car, or even bringing the car to them for a closer look. Serious buyers will typically take one of these steps if they are genuinely interested.

Here, you must emphasize to the customer that your dealership conducts thorough research to offer the best prices and ensures each vehicle undergoes a detailed inspection. This commitment to quality should provide them with peace of mind. While some places may only give cars a quick wash and oil change, we conduct comprehensive 125 to 160-point inspections to ensure top-notch quality.

Furthermore, highlight the value of manufacturer certification, explaining that not every vehicle is certified, and that certification must meet stringent criteria. Purchasing a certified vehicle from the manufacturer provides benefits like free roadside assistance, complimentary oil changes, and extended warranties, which can be worth thousands of dollars. When choosing a certified vehicle, customers retain these valuable benefits and the assurance of quality service.

For the third rebuttal, when a customer says they want to shop around, it's a common reaction. Here's how you can respond: "I understand that you'd like to explore your options. We have a dedicated research team that ensures we offer the best prices within a 500-mile radius. Could you share how far apart we are in terms of pricing?"

When a customer mentions finding a better price elsewhere, calmly address it by explaining that your dealership follows set pricing guidelines. If they claim another dealer is offering the same car at almost half the price, reassure them by saying, "If it seems too good to be true with such a drastic price difference, it's likely due to hidden issues. We all acquire vehicles for similar prices, so such a significant gap raises concerns about the quality and authenticity of the offer." Remember, it's not just about selling the car; it's about selling the experience and building a lasting connection with the customer.

Next, when a customer says, "I want to consult with my bank," it's common. You can respond by highlighting the dealership's extensive experience in securing financing: "I understand your need to discuss this with your bank but remember, we handle financing transactions regularly and can secure better buy rates due to our frequent partnerships. It's like buying T-shirts in bulk; the more we work with a bank, the better rates we receive compared to individual transactions."

Another thing you can do is explain the concept of simple interest loans and the flexibility they offer. You might say, "In the U.S., most dealers utilize simple interest loans, ensuring you only pay interest on the amount you utilize. There's no prepayment penalty, giving you the option to refinance with your bank or credit union for potential savings. This way, you can benefit from better rates and manage your payments efficiently."

When a customer expresses hesitation about making quick decisions, empathize with their approach and gently nudge them toward a decision. Tell them that seizing the opportunity promptly is essential. While there's no pressure, it's important to act swiftly, especially when considering limited availability.

Ask them how long they need to think about their decision. If they say one day, two days, or even a week, suggest a practical approach. Offer them the option to secure the vehicle for 24 hours with a $500 refundable deposit. This helps filter out genuinely interested customers from those who are indecisive or not fully committed to the purchase.

By creating a sense of urgency without undue pressure, you convey the significance of acting decisively when presented with a favorable deal.

For customers hesitant about the financing rate, propose a solution. Offer to proceed with a cashable contract based on your rate. If they prefer to use their bank's financing, they can provide a check within 48 hours. This approach ensures clarity and flexibility for the customer while maintaining a level of commitment to the deal.

If a customer simply says, "***I don't like the color***," then you can take a simplified approach to let them know what you offer. We all have color preferences, and color matters when buying a car. Trust me; people tend to stick to their preferences.

If you don't have that specific color in stock, ask if the customer prefers light or dark colors. Offer to find a color they want if they're willing to buy today. You can also provide a discount or incentive to take the in-stock color. For white cars specifically, mention safety benefits like better visibility at night.

The last rejection (but not the least) we hear from clients is, "***My car is paid off.***" Your response to this should start by presenting enticing options for an upgrade. Offer more value than the current car the customer has, along with additional perks like roadside assistance and maintenance. The idea of trading up to a newer vehicle with benefits such as a warranty and improved features can be appealing.

Your words should encourage the customer to consider the whole situation and make a decision right away. As a salesperson, you can help the customer see the value in making a change. If they are open to trading in their car, the possibility of receiving cash toward their new purchase can be a compelling factor.

In all these counteroffers, don't forget to keep the conversation simple and focused on finding the best deal for the potential customer. This can lead to a successful and satisfying car purchase experience, and you may earn a loyal customer. Dealing with customer concerns can be tough in sales. It's important to have good comebacks to handle these issues confidently and close deals successfully. A helpful team or resources can assist you in tackling objections and improving your sales skills. With reliable guidance and support, you can handle objections smoothly and enhance your performance over time.

For newcomers in the sales industry, I know starting a sales career might seem daunting, but with the right tools and assistance, you can begin your journey toward success. Overcoming objections and using them to your advantage is a big part of being successful in sales.

Here's a piece of advice: work hard, practice, and follow the guidance provided here. You can improve your sales skills and thrive in your career.

NOTES:

Join Drive to Success for Continued Education

Remember it is not the way you start but the way you finish, and you Can write your own paycheck, the choice is yours.

Stick to the process. The turtle wins the race. Remember to go slow and steady, don't rush.

Always ask for Referrals!

Remind your customer to not confuse urgency with pressure.

Always remember that it's 90% you and 10% the product so no matter whether you're selling cars or widgets, you can apply these techniques. It's about the experience and if the experience is good the results will be rewarding.

You are the best of the best you can do it!

When you walk into a closed room, hold your head high like you own the place.

You control your own destiny, everything you put out you get back.

WIN WIN WIN...... you can do it!

Note From the Author,

"We would like to take a moment to express our sincere gratitude for purchasing *Drive to Success*. Your support means the world to us, and we are truly thankful for your trust in our work. Every purchase enables us to continue our mission of educating and inspiring individuals like you.

Thank you once again for being a part of this journey. We are deeply appreciative of your support."

With gratitude,

Jinetta Brown.

Also don't forget to join the VIP list at:

drivetosuccessallstars.com

Made in the USA
Columbia, SC
17 February 2025

53966026R00048